CONFRONTING BROKENNESS IN THE CHURCH

Study by Joshua Hearne
Commentary by Judson Edwards

Free downloadable Teaching Guide for this study available at
NextSunday.com/teachingguides

NextSunday Resources
6316 Peake Road
Macon, Georgia 31210-3960
1-800-747-3016
©2019 by NextSunday Resources
All rights reserved.

TABLE OF CONTENTS

Confronting Brokenness in the Church

HOW TO USE THIS STUDY

NextSunday Resources Adult Bible Studies are designed to help adults study Scripture seriously within the context of the larger Christian tradition and, through that process, find their faith renewed, challenged, and strengthened. We study the Scriptures because we believe they affect our current lives in important ways. Each study contains the following three components:

Study Guide

Each study guide lesson is arranged in four movements:

Reflecting recalls a contemporary story, anecdote, example, or illustration to help us anticipate the session's relevance in our lives.

Studying is centered on giving the biblical material in-depth attention while often surrounding it with helpful insights from theology, ethics, church history, and other areas.

Understanding helps us find relevant connections between our lives and the biblical message.

What About Me? provides brief statements that help unite life issues with the meaning of the biblical text.

Commentary

Each study guide lesson is accompanied by an additional, in-depth commentary on the biblical material. Written by a different author than the study guide, each commentary gives the opportunity for learners to approach the Scripture text from a separate but complementary viewpoint.

Teaching Guide

In addition to the provided study guide and commentary, *NextSunday Resources* also provides a *free* downloadable teaching guide, available at NextSunday.com. Each teaching guide gives the teacher tools for focusing on the content of each study guide lesson through additional commentary and Bible background information. Through teacher helps and teaching options, each teaching guide also provides substance for variety and choice in the preparation of each lesson.

NextSunday
Resources

STUDY INTRODUCTION

Paul left the church a treasure in the letter he wrote to the Christian community in Corinth—the letter we call 1 Corinthians. Sure, Paul was writing with a first-century audience in mind and likely assumed that the second coming of Christ was imminent, but we still benefit from the teachings we find in this letter. By reading it, we gain a rare glimpse not only of Paul's teachings on how to be the church, but also of the difficulties our brothers and sisters of the first century faced.

We should avoid the temptation to dismiss this book as merely a record of a church that once was and is no longer. The words of Paul reach across the centuries to call us to repentance and unity. As Paul struggles with his beloved brothers and sisters who have failed time and again in Corinth, we can easily hear how Paul might struggle with us even today. Paul's original audience struggled with divisions, arguments, jealousy, and sin. They debated what to believe and how to live. The church in Corinth was pressed in on all sides. It was fragile and given to quarreling. In many ways, the Corinthian Christians were struggling even to remember the most basic things Paul had taught them about following their Lord Jesus.

Yet Paul refused to write off these beloved brothers and sisters. Instead, he wrote them a letter in which he promised his undying love for them, even going so far as to name them as his children. Through all of their failures, Paul refused to abandon them to the world, for in them dwelled the spark of God's love that Paul had seen work miracles in many places. Paul confronted the brokenness of this beloved church in Corinth. It was a congregation that was still worth fighting for.

Such a timeless message is fresh and relevant in Christian communities all over the world who are also worth fighting for. With Paul, we learn to confront the brokenness of our beloved church.

PRACTICING
HUMILITY

1 Corinthians 1:18-31

Central Question

Am I too impressed with my own credentials?

Scripture

1 Corinthians 1:18-31 The message of the cross is foolishness to those who are being destroyed. But it is the power of God for those of us who are being saved. 19 It is written in scripture: *I will destroy the wisdom of the wise, and I will reject the intelligence of the intelligent.* 20 Where are the wise? Where are the legal experts? Where are today's debaters? Hasn't God made the wisdom of the world foolish? 21 In God's wisdom, he determined that the world wouldn't come to know him through its wisdom. Instead, God was pleased to save those who believe through the foolishness of preaching. 22 Jews ask for signs, and Greeks look for wisdom, 23 but we preach Christ crucified, which is a scandal to Jews and foolishness to Gentiles. 24 But to those who are called—both Jews and Greeks—Christ is God's power and God's wisdom. 25 This is because the foolishness of God is wiser than human wisdom, and the weakness of God is stronger than human strength. 26 Look at your situation when you were called, brothers and sisters! By ordinary human standards not many were wise, not many were powerful, not many were from the upper class. 27 But God chose what the world considers foolish to shame the wise. God chose what the world considers weak to shame the strong. 28 And God chose what the world considers low-class and low-life—what is considered to be nothing—to reduce what is considered to be something to nothing. 29 So no human being can brag in God's presence. 30 It is because of God that you are in Christ Jesus. He became wisdom from God for us. This means that he made us righteous and holy, and he delivered us. 31 *This is consistent with what was written: The one who brags should brag in the Lord!*

Reflecting

Jim Elliot was a talented and passionate young man with an intense focus and clear calling. This focus and calling led him to study Greek so he could translate the Scripture into other languages. It pushed him to set aside denominational politics and concerns. It challenged him to declare his intention to be a conscientious objector if drafted to serve in the Korean War. All of his interests and passions were subjected to his desire to serve the kingdom of God by traveling to another people, living among them, and sharing the gospel with them.

Jim Elliot ended up serving as a missionary in Ecuador. He began his work among the Quichua people. Eventually, however, he felt called to serve with and among a people he knew as the Auca (who called themselves the Huaorani or Waodani). So Jim and some of his colleagues began eating with, learning the language of, and building relationships with the Auca people. The Auca remained guarded and mistrusting of the foreign missionaries, but Jim and his colleagues began building bridges that spanned the distance between the Auca and the gospel.

The language barrier was a significant challenge, however, and left the missionaries unprotected when several of the Auca sneaked into their camp at night and brutally murdered them. Jim had spent his life finding a way to give of himself to a people who didn't know him and found it hard to trust him. It's not hard to see how some might call his death a waste or foolish. Yet his family read the following in his journal when they received it weeks later: "He is no fool who gives what he cannot keep to gain that which he cannot lose" (Elliot, 144). Years later, others ventured to serve among the Auca and found that the seed that Jim and the others had planted was still there. Imagine their surprise when some of those who had slain Jim and his colleagues repented and were converted.

Studying

Strabo was a first-century Greek historian, geographer, and philosopher. In his *Geography*, he quotes a common proverb about the city of Corinth: "Not for every man is the voyage to Corinth" (para. 3). Strabo explains that this proverb was common because of the temple of the goddess Aphrodite that was in Corinth. This temple is said to have had more than a thousand temple slaves and prostitutes. It was crowded with the wealthy and those who were willing to take part in the trade of flesh for money. Sea captains advised their crews to avoid the temple if they wanted to keep any of their pay as their ships arrived in the port city of Corinth. Many of those same captains, however, squandered incredible amounts of money there themselves.

Paul wrote this letter in a context similar to what Strabo described, and only a few decades later. This Greek port city had been conquered by Rome and made subject to imperial rulers, drafts, and taxes. Latin, the common language of the Roman Empire, never truly supplanted Greek in this city despite its Roman rulers and legions. The city maintained a Greek heart and soul.

First Corinthians is Scripture—and has been for many hundreds of years—but when first written, it was simply a letter sent from Paul to the Christian community he had planted in the heart of Corinth. Paul clearly had a great deal of affection for this congregation and its efforts to be the kingdom of God in Corinth, even as he recognized the special challenges they faced.

This collection of marginalized and persecuted people represented the kingdom of God in a city all too familiar with the powerful, wise, intelligent, and influential. So it seems appropriate that Paul should begin his letter to this beloved community by encouraging them in the peculiar task to which they were called: to represent a different way of living that emphasized sacrifice, love, grace, forgiveness, and mercy. Addressing the secret fears of his brothers and sisters in Corinth, Paul tells them, in effect, "Yes, I know that some may call it foolish, but to those of us who understand the kingdom, the message of the cross is the most powerful thing there is."

In the lines that follow, Paul subtly and slowly subverts the classic and, at the time, common understandings of wisdom and foolishness. That is to say, he suggests that the Christians don't misunderstand power and wisdom, but rather it is the world that has it backwards. At first, Paul does this by insisting that the God of the Christians has already destroyed the wisdom of the wise and rejected the intelligence of the intelligent (1 Cor 1:19), as if to say that human ideas about wisdom and foolishness are nonsensical if backed up by nothing more than consensus or common knowledge.

If that wasn't enough, Paul goes on to encourage the Corinthian Christians to be brave by calling out the wisest and most eloquent opponents that the world has to offer and then dismissing them without even so much as naming them or hearing what they might have to say. Paul then asks, "Hasn't God made the wisdom of the world foolish?" (v. 20). In essence, the Apostle questions whether it really matters what the world may say about wisdom when they've already proven they just don't get it.

> When have you observed "worldly" understandings of wisdom at work in the church? How can believers address this temptation while remaining humble?

Following on this message of encouragement and zealous confidence, Paul goes on to remind the Corinthian community what is at the heart of Christian teaching, what he has called the "message of the cross" (v. 18). Namely, he writes, "we preach Christ crucified" (v. 23). Paul affirms that this Christ is "God's power and God's wisdom" (v. 24). Yet Paul still doesn't shrink away from the perceived foolishness of this message. Rather, he leans into it and suggests that wisdom, intelligence, and influence cannot save the world from itself. Perhaps a "foolish" salvation is precisely what we need—perhaps we need trust and faith more than eloquence, confidence, and brilliance (v. 21).

Finally, Paul discloses the ingenious nature of God's "foolish" plan in verses 26-31. He asks the members of the Corinthian congregation to consider their own place within the big and influential city in which they find themselves.

Paul reminds them that they are not a people who have come from influence, wealth, power, or strength. Rather, they come from weakness, and yet God has done great things through them. God has not done these things *because* of who and what they are, but *in spite* of it. This seems to be the heart of what Paul is driving at in this stirring "pep talk." "Oh no," Paul seems to say, "folks aren't expecting you to change Corinth—that's why it's going to be so great when God uses you to proclaim our 'foolish' message to any who will take a second or two to listen."

The place of the church, Paul suggests in this passage, is that of humble confidence in the goodness and wisdom of God. Believers must not rely on their own goodness or wisdom. By working with powerless, common people, God receives all the glory while the people are remade in the image of God's crucified Son. In that image, they bring the kingdom of God into the world.

> Humility, therefore, is absolutely necessary if man is to avoid acting like a baby all his life. To grow up means, in fact, to become humble, to throw away the illusion that I am the center of everything and that other people only exist to provide me with comfort and pleasure. (Merton, 71)

God has chosen to lead God's people on a path of salvation that the world calls foolish, but the world has already demonstrated—and the city of Corinth has confirmed to the believers who live there—that it doesn't know anything about salvation. In short, although the way of the cross may seem foolish by human standards, Christians have seen their world redefined by the life, death, and resurrection of Jesus. As Paul puts it, "It is because of God that you are in Christ Jesus. He became wisdom from God for us. This means that he made us righteous and holy, and he delivered us" (v. 30).

Understanding

This passage is a powerful way for Paul to introduce a letter that is, at times, quite critical of the fledgling community of

Christians in Corinth. Paul is resolute in proclaiming the message about the cross in crystal-clear terms. He wants there to be no misunderstanding between him and his beloved brothers and sisters in Corinth about the nature of the gospel.

Paul therefore seeks to establish firmly the importance of this "foolish" gospel among those from whom he is separated by many miles. Paul redefines wisdom and foolishness for the Corinthian community. In so doing, he confirms their faith.

Nearly 2,000 years later, it is still important for us to understand at least two essential points in this text. First, the way of the cross may still seem foolish in our contemporary settings. Faith is ultimately a matter of trust and hope. It is not something that depends entirely upon reason or intellect. This is not to say that we should divorce our faith from reason and intellect, but rather that we must understand the limitations of those tools. Even a reasonable faith cannot be reduced to reason alone.

Second, we must understand that God is glorified by working through our weakness. The first step in confronting brokenness in the church, the title of this unit of study, is to recognize that this brokenness is going to be with us, no matter what. As such, we should not be ashamed of our weakness or our inability to do everything by ourselves. After all, God has chosen to do the greatest of works with and among human beings, who are broken and marred by sin and death. God has rejected the strong in favor of the weak. Our faith in God's strength gives room for God to be glorified in our limitations.

> How can practicing humility create a healthier church environment?

What About Me?

• *The message of the cross may seem foolish, but that depends on one's perspective.* Paul encourages us to consider that what may appear either foolish or wise may have more to do with our preconceived notions than it does with the actual truth of the matter. Jesus' life, death, and resurrection may seem foolish or a waste to some, but to Christians, these are saving deeds. They are a clear demonstration of how God chooses to act in, and save, the world.

• *Ultimately, faith is about trusting.* Though reason and intellect may help us to explore our faith and may be a means by which we can worship or experience God, these things cannot carry us into the presence of God by themselves. Rather, we must pair our intellectual pursuits with a trusting and hopeful faith if we want to understand how "Christ crucified" is a message worth proclaiming and depending on.

• *Look at your own situation when you were called.* Paul encourages the Corinthian Christians to keep their own role in the church in mind when they reflect on the foolishness and wisdom of the gospel. We should regularly do the same. How has God used you recently? How is God using you now? These are relevant and significant clues as to how God might be preparing to use you in the future. God doesn't call the qualified, God qualifies the called. What you have been experiencing lately might be God getting you ready for what's coming.

• *There's little room for boasting within the church.* We are servants of a great and glorious God who does great things with, and in spite of, our weaknesses and failures. Therefore, we should only boast if we can do it in a way that gives God the glory that God deserves.

Resources

Elisabeth Elliot, *Shadow of the Almighty: The Life and Testament of Jim Elliot* (Peabody MA: Hendrickson, 1958).

Thomas Merton, *The New Man* (New York: Burns & Oates, 1976).

Strabo, *Geography*, 8.6.20 (26 February 2012)
<http://www.mycrandall.ca/courses/pauline/images/StraboCor.htm> (11 March 2013).

PRACTICING HUMILITY

1 Corinthians 1:18-31

Introduction

Once upon a time, a man died. When he got to heaven, he insisted that he wanted to spend eternity with like-minded Christians. So, God tried to accommodate his request. The man was handed over to a kind interrogator who asked him questions in order to put him in a place in heaven with people just like himself.

"Are you Protestant or Catholic?" the interrogator began.

"Protestant," the man responded.

"Denomination?" the interrogator continued.

"Baptist," the man said.

"Which kind of Baptist—Northern, Southern, Primitive, American, Foot-washing, Freewill, or other?"

"Southern," the man said.

And then the interrogator unleashed a barrage of other choices: Moderate or Fundamentalist? Pro-abortion or anti-abortion? Pro-gay or anti-gay? Republican or Democrat? Pro-cloning or anti-cloning? Praise music or hymns?

By the time the interrogator had finished all of his questions and the man had given all of his answers, the man was escorted to a broom closet where all of the people like him numbered exactly zero!

There is no shortage of issues to divide Christians, is there? If we had to attend church with people exactly like us, we could hold our service in that broom closet. According to the New Testament, this is not a new phenomenon. Just twenty years after Jesus' death and resurrection, the church in Corinth was divided into groups: "My brothers and sisters, Chloe's people gave me some information about you, that you're fighting with each other" (1 Cor 1:11). There was a Paul clique, an Apollos clique, a Peter clique, and a Jesus clique. A mere twenty years into the Christian movement, there were factions everywhere.

So, Paul wrote his first letter to the church in Corinth to speak to this disunity and conflict. For the next five lessons, we will listen in on his words of wisdom to this church in turmoil. On the more-than-slight chance that our own churches are mired in disunity and conflict, his words will likely seem amazingly relevant and insightful.

The God We Never Expected

Paul begins his discourse on dealing with church conflict with some thoughts about power. In our focal passage for this lesson, he reminds us that we have a surprising God we never expected, a God who uses a surprising kind of power we never anticipated.

Several years ago, I read an intriguing book titled *The Pinball Effect* by James Burke (New York: Back Bay, 1997). The book is about some of the serendipities that have taken place in history, quirky surprises that have changed the world—the unexpected interactions between people separated by space and time that ultimately led to the world we know.

It is fascinating to discover all of the strange and unexpected things that have happened in history, things that have had a profound impact on our lives. But when Paul wrote to the Corinthians, he wrote about a historical surprise that makes all of the others seem trivial. History has revealed a God we never expected. The One who fashioned the oceans, flung the stars into the sky, and breathed life into human beings is not at all the kind of God we would have predicted. History has shown us a surprising God. God's story, as revealed in the New Testament, has at least four big surprises in it.

God, the Peasant

First, *the New Testament shows us a God who showed up in human history as a man*. Furthermore, he was not a man who was a king but rather a Galilean peasant.

The Jews had a long history of waiting for their Messiah, and they had a clear idea of what their Messiah would look like when he came. He would be strong, regal, military, and impressive. He would reestablish Israel as the preeminent nation in the world. The Messiah would be a new King David, intent on restoring Israel's glory.

But what Israel (and the world) got was Jesus: a blue-collar worker and a lover of outcasts and sinners, who had no place to lay his head. Jesus was not the Messiah anyone expected. He was the "un-Messiah." He had almost none of the attributes people were expecting.

No one in his right mind would have guessed that God would show up in human history as a lowly peasant, born in a cattle stall, despised by both religious and political authorities, and eventually executed as a common criminal.

When God entered history as a Galilean peasant, no one saw it coming.

God, the Servant

Second, *the New Testament shows us a God who was a servant.* Jesus came into the world with a shocking agenda. He would not rule people; he would serve them.

Jesus stood in the synagogue in Nazareth and announced his game plan: *"The Spirit of the Lord is upon me, because the Lord has anointed me. He has sent me to preach good news to the poor, to proclaim release to the prisoners and recovery of sight to the blind, to liberate the oppressed, and to proclaim the year of the Lord's favor"* (Lk 4:18-19). Jesus did not come into the world to be served but to serve and, eventually, to give his life as a ransom for all.

Jesus' symbol of power was not a sword nor a gavel. It was a towel, which he used to wash the dusty feet of his disciples. The image of a God bending to wash people's feet is almost impossible to conjure, but that is precisely the image Jesus gives us. And because Jesus revealed God to be a servant, he unleashed into the world the notion that serving others is the goal of life. If the God of the universe became a servant and washed feet, shouldn't we humans do the same?

When God entered history as a gentle servant, no one saw it coming.

God, the Sufferer

Third, *the New Testament shows us a God who suffered.* The first two surprises were shocking: the fact that God would show up in human history as a Galilean peasant and the fact that God would serve people were shocking revelations, to say the least. But the fact that God would suffer and die for humanity is almost beyond belief.

In 1 Corinthians 1, Paul acknowledges this reality. Many would simply find a suffering God unthinkable. Many Jews would find this concept a stumbling block, and many Gentiles would find this concept foolish. But, for those who have the faith to accept it, this suffering concept of God is the very power and wisdom of God.

Paul asserts that God's power is a suffering kind of power. It is not right-handed, military, political, financial power. It is left-handed, compassionate, serving, suffering power. It is not the kind of power we would expect the God of the universe to wield, but according to Paul, it is precisely the kind of power Jesus revealed God to have.

Ever since Jesus, humanity has had to think about power in a different way. Power is not merely about clout, strength, and force. It is also about love, sacrifice, and dying. There are different kinds of power, and God (and God's people) have an affinity for the left-handed variety.

God, the Includer

Fourth, *the New Testament shows us a God who includes ordinary people in building the kingdom.* Paul urges the Corinthian believers to think about where they've come from:

> Look at your situation when you were called, brothers and sisters! By ordinary human standards not many were wise, not many were powerful, not many were from the upper class. But God chose what the world considers foolish to shame the wise. God chose what the world considers weak to shame the strong.

And God chose what the world considers low-class and low-life—what is considered to be nothing—to reduce what is considered to be something to nothing. (1 Cor 1:26-28)

The treasure of God was placed in ordinary clay pots (2 Cor 4:7), and that means two practical things for those of us who believe it. First, it means that God is actually able to use us—with all of our foolishness, weakness, and sinfulness. Even though we feel inadequate and unqualified, God can use us. Maybe we need to quit hiding behind our excuses, step up to the plate, and do something bold for God.

Second, it means we have to see the people around us as anything but ordinary. In light of God's plan to use the foolish and weak, we need to reevaluate how we think about foolish, weak people. Those foolish, weak people are actually vessels of the treasure of God. Because of the people Jesus chose as his followers and because of the way he loved and valued them, perhaps we should reevaluate our relationships. Because of Jesus, we have to consider that everyone in our lives is a "thought of God" and valued by God.

Conclusion

When we put those four surprises together, we get an unexpected Messiah with an unexpected agenda that aims an expected kind of power at unexpected recipients. Who could have guessed?

Since Paul's primary purpose in writing 1 Corinthians was to address the conflict in the church, why would he begin his letter with this theology lesson about a surprising God? What was Paul's rationale for beginning with a reminder about this unexpected God that both he and the Corinthians served?

I think Paul knew that theology always affects conduct. Paul begins at the right place because our theology inevitably influences how we live. Tell me honestly about your God, and I will be able to tell you much about your life because we are all shaped in the image of our God.

So, before he ever offered a word of advice about dealing with church conflict, Paul wanted to lay down some theological pillars. He was saying, in effect, "Remember, Corinthian

Christians, the kind of God we serve. Ours is a surprising God who revealed himself in Jesus as a peasant, a servant, a sufferer, and a chooser of unimpressive followers. If our God is like this, it has undeniable implications for the way we live together at church. If our God is like this, shouldn't we be like this as well?"

This meant the Corinthians needed to be willing to serve one another, suffer for one another, see the glory of God in one another, and join hands in declaring this amazing God to the people around them. Once he reminded them of this amazing, unexpected God who revealed himself in Jesus, Paul was then able to offer some practical advice on how to get along with others in the church.

History has indeed unfolded in surprising, quirky ways. Reading a book like *The Pinball Effect* helps us realize some of the amazing historical twists and turns that have led to unexpected consequences in the world. But reading the Bible is even more surprising. To think that God is like Jesus—a Galilean peasant, dedicated to serving others, willing to suffer for others, and willing to call and use ordinary people—is incredible.

The Bible is history's most amazing story. And as Paul well knew, that story has the power to change lives. It even has the power to affect how we treat one another when we come to church on Sunday morning.

In the lessons to come, we will see how Paul takes this theology and translates it into specific suggestions for healing the rift at Corinth. Stay tuned.

Notes

Notes

WORKING TOGETHER

1 Corinthians 3:1-9

Central Question

What is my role in the life of my community?

Scripture

1 Corinthians 3:1-9 Brothers and sisters, I couldn't talk to you like spiritual people but like unspiritual people, like babies in Christ. 2 I gave you milk to drink instead of solid food, because you weren't up to it yet. 3 Now you are still not up to it because you are still unspiritual. When jealousy and fighting exist between you, aren't you unspiritual and living by human standards? 4 When someone says, "I belong to Paul," and someone else says, "I belong to Apollos," aren't you acting like people without the Spirit? 5 After all, what is Apollos? What is Paul? They are servants who helped you to believe. Each one had a role given to them by the Lord: 6 I planted, Apollos watered, but God made it grow. 7 Because of this, neither the one who plants nor the one who waters is anything, but the only one who is anything is God who makes it grow. 8 The one who plants and the one who waters work together, but each one will receive their own reward for their own labor. 9 We are God's coworkers, and you are God's field, God's building.

Reflecting

Not far from where the members of our Christian community live is an apartment building that serves as shelter mainly for folks who can't find or afford a better place to live. That is to say, it's mainly the home of our society's most marginalized and neglected people. Our little Christian community has made a commitment to this particular place, but we've repeatedly struggled with some of the deeply rooted injustices we find there.

One particular Saturday a couple of summers back, many of us were spending the day with our friends on that street and in that complex. We visit them and they visit us. In the midst of these relationships, God gives growth to love and community. But this day, we had a different kind of growth in mind: tomatoes.

We were partnering with our brothers and sisters in the complex—at their request and initiative—to plant a garden in their courtyard so they could have fresh vegetables. As we began to pick up shovels and dirty our hands and knees, I began to wonder if we might be better served by holding a seminar on fair rental practices to educate our neighbors, or contacting a local lawyer or home inspector.

As I reflected fretfully, tomato plant in hand, one of my fellow leaders tapped me on the shoulder. Perceiving that my thoughts had drifted to bigger problems, he remarked with a smile, "The first step in saving the world is to plant that tomato. We'll work out the next step in a bit."

I laughed and did as instructed, considering how easy it was to get distracted from the goodness of working together by getting bogged down in the details. Sometimes our congregations do the same thing. We get so focused on what could be done that we forget what we're doing already.

Studying

This lesson's text challenges our understanding of unity, common life, and the role of dissension and disagreement within a community. Before we dive into it, we should consider what leads to Paul's strong words.

In 1 Corinthians 2, Paul reacquaints himself with his beloved community in Corinth and reminds them of their deep connection founded upon and established by the Holy Spirit. From that foundation, he starts to explain that there is most certainly something mysterious and subtle about the way the Spirit moves in their midst and in the midst of all Christian communities. He explains that "no one has known the depths of God except God's Spirit" (1 Cor 2:11). Upon this subtle and mysterious foundation, Paul calls their minds back to his earlier discussion of foolishness and wisdom. He urges them to depend on the Spirit's intercession for understanding, adding, "We have the mind of Christ" (1 Cor 2:16).

Having established the intimate, subtle, and mysterious nature of their calling as a community and their relationship to each other, Paul begins our passage by accentuating his connection with them. Specifically, he calls them his brothers and sisters (3:1).

The attention Paul gives to this personal connectedness is striking, but it doesn't take long for us to recognize why Paul is so emphatic about their closeness: he is about to criticize, rebuke, and correct them. Paul most certainly wants to reinforce the connection he shares with the Corinthian believers because he knows that his words and tone are going to stress those bonds of friendship. Nevertheless, Paul is willing to take that risk because of the serious nature of their ongoing mistakes and failings.

With 1 Corinthians 3:1, Paul reveals the specific problem that he proceeds to address in the following verses: despite the teaching and nurture he has given them, the Corinthian believers are unspiritual, "babies in Christ." Calling them babies was not meant as a compliment. They are immature and spiritually unformed (or perhaps deformed). We can imagine how we would feel if an esteemed Christian leader labeled our congregation as being made up of unspiritual, immature believers. This must have been difficult words for the Corinthian believers to hear, and yet this description was uncomfortably accurate.

Beyond this basic immaturity, Paul goes on to accuse the Corinthian community of arrested spiritual development: "I gave you milk to drink instead of solid food, because you weren't up to it yet. Now you are still not up to it because you are still unspiritual" (vv. 2-3). The word translated "unspiritual" is literally "of the flesh." Elsewhere in Paul's letters, "flesh" has a deeply negative connotation. In essence, he accuses the people not only of being immature and unprepared, but also of still being bound by that which they were called to leave behind: their sinful past lives, affiliations, and concerns.

On the heels of such a crippling criticism as "you are still unspiritual," Paul brings his diagnosis of dysfunction in the community to a quick conclusion. Precisely put, the Christians in Corinth can't get along with each other. On the contrary, they continue to sow dissension and disunity in their midst over what Paul considers relatively trivial matters. For this reason, they are "still unspiritual" and will continue to be so until they stop acting like the rest of the world and "living by human standards" (v. 3).

Quoting one of the major points of dissension within the Corinthian community, Paul points out that even participating in that disagreement is a mark of the underlying problem of spiritual immaturity and unpreparedness. Paul seems to ask, "As long as all this fighting is more important to you than each other, aren't you just like everybody else outside your community?"

The matter Paul examines has to do with an internal conflict in the community that has resulted in the formation of opposing factions. Some express loyalty to Paul, while others express their loyalty to Apollos, a figure whose credentials Paul seems to be aware of, but uneager to discuss at length (v. 4).

The Corinthians have offered their primary loyalty not to Christ but to human leaders. This confusion over the centrality of Christ, and the conflict it creates, is far more important to Paul than merely resolving a dispute between competing factions or comparing the credentials of favorite preachers. His words of correction, therefore, proceed along those lines. Rather than arguing for his own priority, he subordinates both himself and Apollos to Jesus, who is far superior to both of them.

That is not to say, however, that Paul thinks that he and Apollos have done the same work or are filling the same role in some unimportant way. Rather, he acknowledges that they have both had a role to play in the birth, development, and formation of the Corinthian community. But their roles are insignificant compared to the wonderful mystery that God is working among the Corinthian Christians: growing life in the midst of death and sin and in a place dominated by cultural influences that are opposed to the gospel message.

As such, Paul concludes, "Because of this, neither the one who plants [that is, Paul] nor the one who waters [that is, Apollos] is anything, but the only one who is anything is God who makes it grow" (v. 7). Paul and Apollos are united not by their gifts, roles, or skills, but by their common purpose and their common Lord.

Paul insists that he and Apollos are united in Christ, no matter the petty competitiveness of their Corinthian partisans. They are both God's coworkers (v. 9). They may be compensated differently based on the work they do and how they do it, as Paul suggests in verse 8, but they're on the same team. They share a common purpose of building up the Corinthian community. Therefore, the Corinthians must cease their quarreling. Even if the Paul faction should "win" (whatever that might mean), it would defeat Paul's greater purpose. Indeed, it would defeat the purpose of God, in which both Paul and Apollos share.

> Why is it sometimes difficult to acknowledge the role others have played in reaching a goal?

The Apostle concludes with words of encouragement. Perhaps he realized that he had stepped on toes with his strong rebuke of the Corinthians' factionalism. Despite his deep concerns about the Corinthian believers' immaturity, in verse 9 he nonetheless assures them that they are God's field and God's building. In the verses that follow (vv. 10-17), he explains that this building is, in fact, a holy temple where God dwells.

> How are we reminding ourselves of shared goals that help diminish rivalry or mistrust in an organization?

Understanding

Members of the church today ought to appreciate Paul's practice of careful correction. We should give careful attention to what Paul says and how it applied to his original audience. At the same time, we should ponder how it might also apply to believers today.

First, we should not overlook Paul's foundational assertion that jealousy and quarreling within a congregation is a sign of spiritual immaturity and arrested development. As such, we should take note of Paul's diagnosis for the Corinthian community and consider it in light of our own circumstances.

Jealousy, quarreling, and disunity are symptoms of a deeper problem: inadequate spiritual growth. If we hope to remove jealousy and quarreling from our communities, this will come about by fostering deeper commitment and spiritual formation. It will not be accomplished through political maneuvering or expressions of power or control, no matter how effectively we think we can do this and no matter how much we may want to.

Second, we should pay special attention to Paul's understanding of how to maintain unity in spite of disagreement and conflict. It's not insignificant that Paul subordinates himself in favor of the unity of the Corinthian church. After all, it makes little to no political sense for Paul to make less of his power while he remains geographically distant from Corinth and his perceived opponent is possibly right there on the scene. Yet Paul willingly subordinates himself alongside Apollos. He cites their common purpose and common Lord. Paul placed a priority on unity that eclipsed his need for the praise of his fans.

> Satan always hates Christian fellowship; it is his policy to keep Christians apart. Anything which can divide saints from one another he delights in. He attaches far more importance to godly intercourse than we do. Since union is strength, he does his best to promote separation.
> —C. H. Spurgeon

What About Me?

• *Spiritual immaturity creates big problems.* It may be tempting to believe that our spiritual immaturity is our own problem, but Paul is adamant that immaturity within the community creates big problems for everyone else as well. If our communities need healing, we usually need it individually first.

• *Our congregation isn't meant to be divided.* Though divisions and factions may seem to be business as usual for some congregations, they're not part of how the kingdom of God is supposed to work. Paul takes divisions very seriously, and so should we. Divisions point out our need to continue being converted and formed as followers of Jesus.

• *Each of us plays a role within our community.* As members of a community of Christians, there are things that we can do that others cannot. We are called to do something for the good of the community. Likewise, we are not called to do everything. We should learn to trust and depend on our brothers and sisters to fulfill their own roles.

• *Whatever good we might do, we are only ever joining God in doing good.* It can be tempting to imagine that we are going out and doing good things for God when we serve or find a cause to support. In fact, God is already at work in the world and is already redeeming the world with God's powerful love. What we are doing when we serve is joining God in the places where God is already at work.

• *Being united is better than proving oneself to be right.* Without a doubt, the desire to prove ourselves is one that stems from pride and self-obsession. Unity, however, requires our commitment to love, even at the expense of our own egos and desires. If we're right, we can trust that God will make that clear—if indeed it's necessary for it to be clear.

Resource

Robert Scott Nash, *1 Corinthians*, Smyth & Helwys Bible Commentary (Macon GA: Smyth & Helwys, 2009).

WORKING TOGETHER

1 Corinthians 3:1-9

Introduction

Last lesson we studied 1 Corinthians 1:18-31, a passage that reminded us of the surprising wonder of our God. As Paul described the foolishness of God and the foolishness of the cross, we celebrated the unexpected plan of God to redeem the world through a Galilean peasant who was a servant, who suffered and died, and who chose unlikely, flawed people to establish his kingdom. Last lesson's passage enabled us to rejoice in the character of God as revealed to us by Jesus.

This lesson, though, we're confronted with a more sobering text. In 1 Corinthians 3:1-9, Paul directly addresses the conflict in the Corinthian church. In the first two chapters, he carefully sketched a theology to serve as the foundation for his advice and reminded the Corinthians about a God who entered history to serve and suffer.

But in chapter 3, he moves away from theology and starts addressing the problems in the church. The Corinthian church had more than its share of problems, and Paul begins to confront those problems in our verses for this lesson.

To Live Below with Saints We Know

The sad truth is that the Corinthian church is not the exception. We wish we could see this church as unusually contentious, but it wasn't. To confirm that, all most of us have to do is look back at our own church experience. What many of us see as we examine our past is church fights, church splits, hurt feelings, long business meetings, and pastors who left in a huff. It would seem that most of us have spent our church lives in Corinth.

There is an old poem that goes, "To live above with saints we love, O, that will be glory. To live below with saints we know...well, that's a different story." That old poem is worth repeating because it fits so well with our verses for this lesson. In theory, the church is a wonderful place of harmony and happiness, but in practice, the church is often a contentious place of squabbling and squawking. "Living below with the saints we know" is one of the biggest challenges many of us face.

It seems odd and troubling, really. People who know God and are led by God's Spirit should not be like worldly folks. God's people should be gracious, kind, and generous. But Paul is candid enough to speak the truth: "Brothers and sisters, I couldn't talk to you like spiritual people but like unspiritual people, like babies in Christ. I gave you milk to drink instead of solid food, because you weren't up to it yet. Now you are still not up to it because you are still unspiritual" (1 Cor 3:1-3).

One of the saddest things about church squabbling is that people come to church precisely to escape squabbling. All week long we have to deal with conflict at work, at home, in the neighborhood, and even on the ball field. We are fed up with arguing and want to find an oasis of sanity and serenity in this sea of chaos and contention. So, we come to church and expect harmony and happiness to prevail. We've heard the church sing "We are one in the Spirit, we are one in the Lord" and assume it is more than just a song.

That hope lasts until we go to our first church business meeting or serve on our first committee. Then, we are shocked to discover that the people at church can be every bit as mean and contentious as the people in the office. We realize, to our dismay, that it is much easier to sing words than it is to live them.

Three Ways to Build a Wall

What we discover is what Paul discovered when he looked honestly at the church at Corinth. Paul saw three things in that church that hurt its witness and effectiveness, and he mentioned them specifically in chapter 3.

• *Jealousy*: Paul saw jealousy among the people in Corinth. He doesn't say what they were jealous of, but we all know how easily jealousy can take root in a church. I get jealous because you are on the pastor search committee, and I am not. I get jealous because your child has the lead in the church musical, and mine doesn't. I get jealous because you were elected a deacon, and I wasn't. There is no limit to the number of issues that can make us jealous of one another, and that jealousy begins to plant the seeds of divisiveness.

• *Quarreling*: Paul knew the people in the Corinthian church were quarreling with one another. It's one thing to be jealous; it's another thing altogether to let jealousy become public and lead to church fights. I'm guessing that the church in Corinth had some business meetings in which "good Christians" got red-faced and said some things they later regretted. And I'm guessing that most of us who have been in church all of our lives can remember occasions like that, too.

• *Factions*: Paul also knew that the Corinthian church was divided. He writes that one says, "I belong to Paul" while another says, "I belong to Apollos" (v. 4). In chapter 1, Paul alluded to even more factions in the church: the existence of a Paul group, an Apollos group, a Peter group, and even a Jesus group. Every time the church met, the members of these little groups probably whispered secrets to each other about "those troublemakers in the church." Of course, none of those factions saw itself as the problem.

Any one of those three factors can destroy the unity of a church. Jealousy is insidious. Quarreling is a dead-end street. And splitting into factions sends the church off in different directions, diluting its passion. Each of those factors erects a wall that divides church members from one another.

But what is really sad is that those three factors usually feed on one another. Jealousy leads to quarreling, which leads to factions, which leads to a miserable church experience. Jealousy, quarreling, and factions usually travel together and conspire to destroy church unity. When they crop up, they create a great deal of disillusionment. Those seekers who have come to church to escape the bickering of the world are likely to drop out when they experience bickering here, too. They leave, disappointed that the church wasn't the place of joy and unity they thought it would be.

The Role of the Leader

One thing we dare not miss in this passage is the role of the leader when church conflict arises. Paul gives us an image of a leader with no ego who simply wants to serve, a leader with no agenda other than advancing the kingdom of God: "After all, what is Apollos? What is Paul? They are servants who helped you to believe. Each one had a role given to them by the Lord: I planted, Apollos watered, but God made it grow. Because of this, neither the one who plants nor the one who waters is anything, but the only one who is anything is God who makes it grow" (1 Cor 3:5-7).

There is an old, probably apocryphal story about a priest long ago who was under fire by his parishioners. Many didn't like him and claimed he was incompetent. These disgruntled parishioners took up a petition to get rid of the priest and passed it around among themselves. When the priest heard about the petition, the story goes, he tracked it down...and signed it himself!

I don't know if that story is true, or if it is, how the story ended, but I'm optimistic it had a happy ending. Why? Because that priest didn't have a big ego. He didn't grow defensive; he knew it wasn't about him. That priest knew he had faults and I'm sure often felt overwhelmed by his job. That priest was living in the spirit of 1 Corinthians 3, and any leader who can adopt that attitude can help quell church conflict. He or she may not be able to stop it completely, but a humble, servant spirit goes a long way in putting out the fires of dissension.

All of us who serve as staff members, deacons, committee members, and in other leadership positions in the church have to get over ourselves. It's not about us; it's about God. It's not about exulting in the limelight; it's about serving in the shadows. It's not about being successful so we'll look good; it's about planting and watering so God can bring the increase.

One of the best antidotes to church conflict is a church leader who leads with the right spirit. A no-ego, non-defensive attitude is always contagious, and others in the church begin to catch that spirit, too.

The Big Picture

We always have to keep our eyes fixed on the big picture: "The one who plants and the one who waters work together, but each one will receive their own reward for their own labor. We are God's coworkers, and you are God's field, God's building" (vv. 8-9).

If those of us in the church could just step back and remember our calling, our big purpose, a lot of the issues we argue about would melt away. Who cares how many chairs we buy for the fellowship hall? Who cares what color carpet we get for the youth room? Who cares if the youth minister doesn't keep regular office hours? I know those issues can be divisive, but when placed alongside our purpose, which is to work together to build the kingdom of God, surely those issues need not divide us.

But ego steps up and makes mountains out of those mole-hills. Most church squabbles revolve around the issue of power. What we're really fighting about is not the issue itself but questions such as: Who's in charge here? Who gets to call the shots? Who is going to get their way? When personal power becomes the issue, things like chairs, carpet, and the youth minister's office hours start to loom large. I want *my* way about the chairs, carpet, and youth minister, and I'm going to be upset if I don't get it.

Paul reminds us that it's not about me and my way. We're all pulling on the same rope, striving for the same purpose. We're all followers of Jesus Christ, bound together by a common purpose to love people and love God. If we keep our eyes fixed on that common purpose, we won't let trivial issues sabotage us. We'll be able to sing "one in the spirit, one in the Lord" and actually mean it.

Conclusion

Whenever we find ourselves in the midst of church conflict, we would do well to ponder a list of important questions:
• Am I trying to get my own way in this situation?

• How will this conflict affect those who come to church looking for an oasis of love?
• Have I talked honestly and lovingly to people on "the other side"?
• Has conflict become a way of life for our church?
• Am I talking secretly to people in my group?
• Am I willing to admit that I could be wrong?

Those questions can help us come to grips with our own part in the conflict. Until we're willing to admit that we might be part of the problem in our church, we will continue to throw stones at others, assuming that *they* are the problem. I'm sure each of those factions in the church at Corinth assumed it had the right perspective and needed to rule the roost.

But Paul said no. No one faction gets to rule the roost. We are all in God's field, and God is growing all of us. We are all God's building, and God is constructing all of us. In other words, we're all incomplete, all a work in progress, and all flawed.

So, we all bring our particular perspective, gifts, and talents to the mix. Where I am weak, you are strong. Where I am wrong, you are right. And together, we make an unbeatable team. Together, we are God's servants, building a kingdom of love and grace right where we live.

Notes

Notes

LEADING
BY EXAMPLE

1 Corinthians 4:14-21

Central Question

How can I demonstrate the change I would like to see in my church?

Scripture

1 Corinthians 4:14-21 I'm not writing these things to make you ashamed but to warn you, since you are my loved children. 15 You may have ten thousand mentors in Christ, but you don't have many fathers. I gave birth to you in Christ Jesus through the gospel, 16 so I encourage you to follow my example. 17 This is why I've sent Timothy to you; he's my loved and trusted child in the Lord; he'll remind you about my way of life in Christ Jesus. He'll teach the same way as I teach everywhere in every church. 18 Some have become arrogant as if I'm not coming to see you. 19 But, if the Lord is willing, I'll come to you soon. Then I won't focus on what these arrogant people say, but I'll find out what power they possess. 20 God's kingdom isn't about words but about power. 21 Which do you want? Should I come to you with a big stick to punish you, or with love and a gentle spirit?

Reflecting

Pachomius was conscripted into the Roman legions in AD 310. As Rome trained and prepared him to do the bidding of the emperor, he took shelter in hard places with little in the way of comfort or safety. He did not come from a Christian family or know anything about Christians apart from secondhand rumors. Even so, a group of these hated and supposedly subversive Christians gave him a blanket and some food one night, because they were inspired to do so by their belief in Jesus. He vowed to learn more of their Lord and their ways after he completed his military service.

As soon as his term of service ended, Pachomius sought out some Christians to learn about what they did and believed. In the year 314, he was converted to the way of Jesus and the kingdom of God. Three years later, he began to follow an ascetic monk and hermit named Palaemon. For many years, he imitated Palaemon, thus learning the way of monastic spirituality in the desert. But his life as a hermit was disrupted when God called Pachomius to build a community for monks in the desert of Egypt.

At first, few heeded Pachomius's invitation to join a community of Christians in the harsh desert where they could learn how to pray and love. The Spirit, however, moved in the few who did. Soon, the little monastery had reached its limit, and another was planted.

These were not congregations such as existed in the cities and towns of Egypt. By and large, the monks were not priests—they had no "official" status in the church hierarchy. Yet the Spirit was moving, and soon Pachomius was guiding many who followed Jesus. When Pachomius died in 348, there were nearly 3,000 monasteries throughout Egypt. Each monk had learned the way of disciple-ship by imitating the example of another (Hearne).

> Example is the school of mankind, and they will learn at no other.
> —Kurt Herbert

Studying

Paul encouraged the Corinthian Christians to follow his example (1 Cor 4:16). This exhortation makes much more sense if we read it in connection with the verses that directly precede it in Paul's letter.

The Apostle had just discussed the factions and divisions growing within the Corinthian congregation. He dismissed the reasons for this division as far less important than what should have united them as brothers and sisters, namely, Jesus himself. Furthermore, he subordinates the status not only of his perceived opponent, Apollos, but also of himself and even Peter to the good of the community and the priorities of the kingdom of God.

First Corinthians 4 begins with additional words of exhortation. Paul establishes his own place within God's plan for the congregation at Corinth. He is, he says, a servant of Christ. As such, it is only appropriate for God to judge him (see 1 Cor 4:1, 4). In contrast to this position of humility, Paul turns his attention to the Corinthian community, which is becoming arrogant in its division and conflict (v. 6). He even goes so far as to mockingly refer to them as "rich" and "kings" (v. 8). Paul encourages the Corinthian believers not to get ahead of themselves and think of themselves as greater than they are, since God's judgment is not yet leveled.

Whose example has been an inspiration to you?

To further make his point, Paul widens the gap between how the Corinthians feel about themselves and about how Paul feels about himself (vv. 9-10). This reflection gives way to one of the more common rhetorical techniques Paul employed in his letters: he presents a long list of attributes, heaping one on top of the other, to make his point. The Apostle describes himself as foolish, weak, disreputable, hungry, thirsty, poorly clothed, beaten, homeless, weary, reviled, persecuted, and slandered (vv. 10-13). He ends with a flourish by calling himself and the other apostles "the scum of the earth, the waste that runs off everything" (v. 13).

These verses were fresh in the minds of the original audience as Paul moves on to this lesson's passage. As if he knows the shame that must be growing in the minds of his audience as he taunts them for their arrogance, Paul assures them that his goal is not to shame them with these strong words but rather to correct them as a loving parent. He reminds them that he is the parent of the Corinthian community and they are his beloved children "in Christ Jesus" and "through the gospel" (v. 15).

Paul suggests a distinction between "mentors in Christ" and "fathers" (v. 15) that should not escape our attention. Though he has previously subordinated both himself and Apollos to their common Lord, he may well now be analyzing some essential differences between himself and his perceived opponents. He does not necessarily or maliciously belittle them or their role. Even so, he draws the Corinthian believers' attention toward his own unique role within the life of the community.

This distinction between "mentors" and "fathers" gives Paul the authority to claim what likely sounded just as audacious then as it does now: "Follow my example" or, more literally, "become imitators of me" (4:16). We must recognize that Paul only says this with the memory of verses 10-13 echoing in the Corinthian believers' ears. He is not asking them to copy his clothes, his rhetoric, or his hairstyle. Rather, he is inviting them to participate in the suffering that naturally comes to those who follow in the way of the kingdom of God.

> So a person should think about us this way—as servants of Christ and managers of God's secrets. (1 Cor 4:1)

This isn't a matter of Paul boosting his own ego by creating an entourage of imitators. Rather, it is Paul's prescription for a self-obsessed and spiritually immature community of fledgling Christians. Think of this approach as something like spiritual training wheels. They should follow Paul's example of sacrificial suffering until they are capable of striking out on their own with a similar attitude.

This is precisely why Paul sent Timothy to Corinth. He wanted him to serve as an example to the flagging congregation. Paul calls Timothy "my loved and trusted child in the Lord" (v. 17) much as he calls the Corinthian community his "loved children" (v. 14). This is not a coincidence. Rather, it establishes the family connection that exists between the Corinthian Christians and Timothy. If both the Corinthians and Timothy are Paul's loved children, then the Corinthians must welcome Timothy as their brother.

Timothy is also meant to teach the Corinthians. As Paul explains, "He'll remind you about my way of life in Christ Jesus. He'll teach the same way as I teach everywhere in every church" (4:17). It's as if Paul is trying to say through Timothy's presence,

"You've strayed from what I taught you and what I teach everywhere I go."

This reference to what Paul teaches may refer generally to the "message of the cross" he describes in 1 Corinthians 1:18. It is also possible that it refers to the way of life described in the preceding passages, especially 4:9-13. Regardless, Paul clearly believes it is crucial for the Corinthian Christians to relearn Paul's "way of life in Christ Jesus" (4:17).

Finally, Paul proposes that part of the reason the Corinthian Christians have the confidence to drift away from Paul's teachings is his extended absence from them. He assures them that he plans to return to help correct the community "if the Lord is willing" (v. 19). His plan seems to be to separate those who only talk about the kingdom from those who are actually living it out, since "God's kingdom isn't about words but about power" (v. 20).

He closes this section of his letter with something of an ultimatum. Reminding the Corinthian Christians that he will return to them soon, he asks them if they'd rather have him "with a big stick" to rebuke and correct or "with love and a gentle spirit," that is, with words of comfort and kindness (v. 21). Having laid out the possibilities, he leaves it to them to decide.

Understanding

Paul's invitation for the Corinthians to imitate him and learn a way that depends not on words but on power challenges congregations even today. First, we must pay special attention to the role Paul plays in the life of the Corinthian community. He names himself as "father" but also understands the presence and role of "mentors in Christ" (v. 15). We cannot understand what Paul is trying to accomplish in this passage and how it relates to our lives without first understanding the intimate and robust relationship that existed between Paul and the Corinthian Christians.

Second, we need to understand precisely what Paul challenged the Corinthians to imitate when he told them to follow his example. By virtue of their special relationship, Paul had the authority to ask this of them, but we must steer away from understanding this as an egotistical plea for commitment to Paul. Rather, we should remember the many words Paul used in the preceding chapters to subordinate himself, and loyalty to him, to God. Paul challenges the Corinthians to be imitators of Paul's way of following Jesus, a way that is characterized by sacrifice.

Third, this entire passage—and 1 Corinthians as a whole— makes more sense if we apply Paul's admonition in 4:20 to their interpretation. He writes, "God's kingdom isn't about words but about power." Paul's many corrections, rebukes, and theological explanations are careful demonstrations of this principle. The Apostle is actively pushing the Corinthians to think seriously about the practice of their faith and not merely the words they use to talk about it.

What About Me?

• *We should remember those who have guided our spiritual formation.* Whether they are "fathers," "mentors," teachers, counselors, pastors, or anything else, we should take time to give thanks for those whom God has put in our lives to teach us how better to follow Jesus, love God, and love others.

• *Imitating people we trust and admire is often the first step toward growth.* As we learn how to live out our faith, we often begin by imitating the example of somebody else—somebody we respect and who is more spiritually mature. We're not intended to learn the ways of Jesus and the kingdom by ourselves.

• *We shouldn't imitate just anybody, though.* Paul doesn't say, "Find somebody to imitate." Surely, some who had strayed in Corinth had done so by following someone who wasn't worthy of imitation. Rather, we grow when we imitate those who are following Jesus more closely and more faithfully.

• *We're more likely to learn how to follow Jesus by practice than by reading or thinking.* It can be tempting to believe that if we'll only get all of our "thinking" about God in order, then surely we will be disciples of Jesus. But it seems fairly clear that knowledge alone is not enough. In the Gospels, even the demons rightly recognize who Jesus is. We learn to be disciples by practice and by spending time with others who are also determined to follow Jesus with their whole lives and not merely with their thoughts and words. Spiritual formation is a process best accomplished by and within a Christian community.

Resources

Joshua Hearne, "Pachomius, Monastic, Hermit, Founder of Communities," *Telling the Stories that Matter*, 9 May 2013 < http://www.ttstm.com/2013/05/may-9-pachomius-monastic-hermit-founder.html >.

Robert Scott Nash, *1 Corinthians*, Smyth & Helwys Bible Commentary (Macon GA: Smyth & Helwys, 2009).

LEADING
BY EXAMPLE

1 Corinthians 4:14-21

Introduction

When conflict arises in a church, we have some tools available to help us deal with it.

For one thing, we have an understanding of God that provides a model for our relationships with others. As we saw in 1 Corinthians 1, if God is like Jesus—"foolish" enough to die on the cross (v. 18)—then we ought to be "foolish" enough to serve and sacrifice ourselves. This first lesson of our unit gave us a theological framework for dealing with church conflict. To put it simply, those of us who claim to follow Jesus should behave like Jesus.

But we also have a vision of a kingdom that is bigger than our personal wishes and plans. In our study of 1 Corinthians 3, we heard Paul's reminder that we can be petty and selfish, breaking into cliques and factions, but that our vision should be bigger than that. We should be God's servants, working together to build God's kingdom.

These two tools—a theology of servanthood and a vision of God's kingdom—are essential if we are to deal with the challenges that will inevitably arise in the church.

Our lesson for this lesson from 1 Corinthians 4 gives us a third tool: the importance of flesh-and-blood models of reconciliation. If a picture is worth a thousand words, a living model of grace and kindness is worth at least a million words when a church is divided. In 1 Corinthians 4:14-21, Paul reminds us of the importance of leading by example.

Getting Personal

The reason Paul felt he could help the people in Corinth was simple: he *knew* them. He felt like a father to them. They might have had many spiritual tutors or guardians, but they had had only one "father" (1 Cor 4:15). Paul felt qualified to speak to their situation because he knew them and loved them like a parent.

Caring for each other is always a prerequisite for resolving church disputes. If the members of the church at Corinth had known each other and cared for each other like that, they could have resolved their differences in a heartbeat. When we really know and love the people around us, disputes rarely happen, and when they do happen, we can deal with them before they have time to fester.

But what typically happens when a church is squabbling is that people lose the personal touch and become impersonal. They forget relationships and start focusing on issues, doctrines, ideas, and concepts—and those things are guaranteed to be divisive. We can sit down with almost any person in our church and discover that we don't agree on all issues, doctrines, ideas, and concepts. But if we know that person, those differences won't destroy our relationship. We *know* one another, and we're not going to let our differences come between us.

In effect, Paul was modeling for the church at Corinth what needed to happen among them. They needed to get personal. The Apollos faction needed to have the Paul faction over for supper. The Peter clique needed to go on a picnic with the Jesus clique. The people at Corinth needed to quit looking at their differences and really get to know one another. It's hard to stay mad at someone with whom you've just shared a meal or cracked a joke.

Needed Reminders

All too often, however, those of us in the church forget to be personal with one another. So did the people in the church in Corinth. Therefore, Paul intended to send Timothy to remind them of Paul's ways among them so they would know and love each other the way he knew and loved them. Timothy was to be an ambassador to remind the people of the importance of the personal.

We need those reminders, too. Passages like this one can remind us not to become so consumed with issues, doctrine, ideas, and concepts that we lose sight of love. Our calling as followers of Jesus Christ is not to agree with one another on everything. If we insist on sharing fellowship only with people just like us, we will find ourselves meeting in a broom closet. We *will* have differences and, yes, we *will* have disputes, but those differences and disputes don't have to be fatal. If they happen in the context of love and respect, they might even be beneficial.

Certain passages in the Bible (for example, Eph 4:1-16) can give us needed reminders that unity is possible despite our differences. But there are other reminders that can come, too, and some of them come with a certain amount of pain.

• *Personal disillusionment.* Our own disillusionment with church can drive us to change. If we've been in the midst of a church dispute long enough, we might eventually tire of it and start considering the possibility that we need to do things a different way. Surely, church is not supposed to be like this. Surely, God has something better in store for our family of faith. Personal disillusionment can be a much-needed reminder to us that we—and our church—need to change.

• *The people slipping out the back door.* Those people coming to church to find an oasis of love and unity can also remind us of our calling as a church. When we see families quietly slipping out the back door never to return again, it should be a major wake-up call. Do we really want to be a stumbling block in the path of people trying to find a place of love? Do we really want to be just like the world in our strife and contention? Or can we use the disillusionment of others as motivation for change?

• *Models of kindness and grace.* In nearly every church dealing with conflict, there is at least one person who has a gracious, conciliatory spirit. This person has no axe to grind, endeavors to know and love people on both sides of the dispute, and remains, in the words of family systems expert Edwin Friedman, "a non-anxious presence." I assume that's exactly the role Paul wanted Timothy to play in the Corinthian conflict. One role model is worth a million words. Sometimes one role model is all it takes for us to decide to become role models, too.

Whatever it takes—Scripture, personal disillusionment, people defecting from our church, or the presence of a "Timothy" among us—we need to be reminded of our calling as the people of God.

Beyond Words

"I encourage you to follow my example," Paul wrote to the Corinthians (1 Cor 4:16). To remind them of who he was and how he lived in the ways of Christ, he sent Timothy to instruct them. Timothy was coming to them not to talk but to live. He was their flesh-and-blood example of peace and reconciliation. Paul even went on to say that talk is inadequate: "God's kingdom isn't about words but about power" (v. 20). What the church in Corinth needed was the same thing our churches need when we're dealing with conflict: individuals who lead by example and are models of grace.

The Old Testament story of Ruth and Naomi is a classic example of the power of leading by example and the persuasiveness of a good role model. The most famous line in the story is the one we usually hear quoted at weddings: "Wherever you go, I will go; and wherever you stay, I will stay. Your people will be my people, and your God will be my God" (Ruth 1:16).

Ruth made that commitment to her mother-in-law, Naomi. If you think about it, it was an evangelistic moment. "Your God will be my God." Why? Why would Ruth want Naomi's God? I think it was because she had been with Naomi, had observed the way she handled her grief, and had received her kindness day after day. She chose Naomi's God because she had already chosen Naomi. Ruth had been persuaded, I think, by the power of a life well lived.

Jim Ellenwood, one of the early leaders of the YMCA, said that one of the most influential moments in his life happened one night when he was a young boy. He said his bedroom door was cracked open that night, and he saw his father come out of the bedroom, where there was no heat, in order to be by the fireplace in the living room. He watched as his father knelt by the fireplace to pray before he went to bed. His father had no idea anyone was watching; this was just his nightly routine. But

Jim Ellenwood said that the unspoken witness of his father influenced him more than all of the sermons on faith and prayer he would hear the rest of his life. It was simple, quiet, and real.

A long time ago, a preacher named Horace Bushnell preached a sermon he called "Unconscious Influence" (*Sermons for New Life*, rev. ed. [New York: Scribner's, 1876] 186–205). In that sermon, he said every person has an influence that emanates from him or her just as surely as a certain fragrance emanates from a rose. Bushnell said that it is this unconscious influence that really guides people. The way to be a witness for Christ, he said, is to have an unconscious influence that is authentically loving.

He was talking about the same thing Paul had in mind in our verses for this lesson. Paul was willing to be a model for the Corinthians. He wanted Timothy to be a model for them. Especially, he wanted them to be models for one another. Paul knew it was their unconscious influence that would really make a difference in the life of their church.

In the final analysis, words are inadequate when addressing contentious issues. A series of sermons or Sunday school lessons on church conflict might help a little, but those words can only go so far. They will pale in effectiveness beside the best answer for church conflict anyone has yet discovered: a few gracious people who will lead by example and let the fragrance of grace start to permeate the entire church.

Conclusion

Paul concludes this section of his letter with a question: "Should I come to you with a big stick to punish you, or with love and a gentle spirit?" (v. 21).

Paul was planning a trip to Corinth, if the Lord willed, and wanted to know what kind of attitude he should show up with. Certainly, he had the capacity to show up with a stick. Paul could be tough when necessary. He was known to be both blunt and critical. Paul had approached more than one person or church with a stick.

But he wanted to come to Corinth with love in a spirit of gentleness. He wanted the Corinthians to start being personal with one another, get rid of their cliques, quit playing power games, and resolve their differences. He wanted them to work together in love to build the kingdom of God right there where they lived, worked, and went to church. Then he could visit them not to reprove them, but to rejoice with them.

What about our own church situations? Does someone need to show up with a stick to chide us or shame us into changing our ways? Do we have to call in outside mediators and experts to do what we should have done ourselves? Do we have to go through intolerable pain before we can repent and become a place of unity?

Or can we do what Paul wanted the Corinthians to do? Can we start being personal with one another, getting to know each other, and spending time together? Can we get rid of our factions and quit talking in our little groups? Can we quit playing power games and see beyond our own egos? Can we resolve our differences—or at least learn to respect each other in spite of our differences?

Let's hope we can. And let's each vow to be that person who quietly and gently serves as a model of grace for the entire church.

Notes

Notes

DEMANDING
ACCOUNTABILITY

1 Corinthians 5:1-13

Central Question

What should accountability look like in my church?

Scripture

1 Corinthians 5:1-13 Everyone has heard that there is sexual immorality among you. This is a type of immorality that isn't even heard of among the Gentiles—a man is having sex with his father's wife! 2 And you're proud of yourselves instead of being so upset that the one who did this thing is expelled from your community. 3 Though I'm absent physically, I'm present in the spirit and I've already judged the man who did this as if I were present. 4 When you meet together in the name of our Lord Jesus, I'll be present in spirit with the power of our Lord Jesus. 5 At that time we need to hand this man over to Satan to destroy his human weakness so that his spirit might be saved on the day of the Lord. 6 Your bragging isn't good! Don't you know that a tiny grain of yeast makes a whole batch of dough rise? 7 Clean out the old yeast so you can be a new batch of dough, given that you're supposed to be unleavened bread. Christ our Passover lamb has been sacrificed, 8 so let's celebrate the feast with the unleavened bread of honesty and truth, not with old yeast or with the yeast of evil and wickedness. 9 I wrote to you in my earlier letter not to associate with sexually immoral people. 10 But I wasn't talking about the sexually immoral people in the outside world by any means—or the greedy, or the swindlers, or people who worship false gods—otherwise, you would have to leave the world entirely!

11 But now I'm writing to you not to associate with anyone who calls themselves "brother" or "sister" who is sexually immoral, greedy, someone who worships false gods, an abusive person, a drunk, or a swindler. Don't even eat with anyone like this. 12 What do I care about judging outsiders? Isn't it your job to judge insiders? 13 God will judge outsiders. *Expel the evil one from among you!*

Reflecting

Accountability with the community of faith is something Christians have struggled with from the very beginning. Nobody can deny the need for correction and, at times, painful reformation within the lives of congregations and individuals. We live in a broken world, and our communities are made of sinners who, at their core, are afflicted with a tragic self-obsession. Yet, at the same time, it can be difficult to enact "church discipline" within our congregations because it can feel exclusive, punishing, and vindictive. Many of us may have stories of "church discipline" gone wrong and relationships brutally severed in search of congregational "purity" and "rightness."

When we turn to the history of the church and its people to help us understand this tricky subject, we find there are many examples. But that's precisely the problem—we have stories on both sides!

We have the story of Abba Moses of Ethiopia, who carried a leaking sack of sand to a meeting in the monastery to determine how to punish a brother who had committed some offense. When he arrived, the brothers asked him about the sack. He remarked, "My sins run out behind me, and I do not see them, and today I am coming to judge the errors of another" ("Stories of the Desert Fathers"). Stories like this remind us never to be in a hurry to pass judgment on the sins of a brother or sister in Christ.

At the same time, however, we also have the record of beautiful communities bound together by their accountability to one

> Correct him, but not as a foe, nor as an adversary exacting a penalty, but as a physician providing medicines.
> —John Chrysostom

another. We cannot overlook the deep bonds forged in account-ability and discipline that we see in the Confessing Church in Germany under Nazi domination and in the Celtic and Egyptian monastic movements.

How, then, do we walk the delicate balance between account-ability and exclusion? Perhaps our brother Paul can tell us.

Studying

At the end of 1 Corinthians 4, Paul challenges the Corinthian Christians to imitate his way of following Jesus. He invites them to take up the way that proclaims "Christ crucified" instead of the way that proclaims themselves to be elevated and powerful. This is a hard sell for the divided and fractured community, so Paul must resort to reminding them that he will be returning to them sooner than they expect and that he can come with strong words and rebuking or with comforting and gentle words.

Paul insists that the kingdom of God depends on "power" or action rather than talk (1 Cor 4:20). By turning the thoughts of his audience away from talk and toward their actions, Paul not only primes his audience for his rebuke of their ungodly behavior in chapter 5, he also transitions deftly into it.

As Paul wades into this discussion of sexual immorality and the Corinthian believers' dysfunctional reaction to it, you can almost sense that he has been waiting to bring up this topic but looking for the right opportunity. He writes with an incredulous tone. It is as if he can barely believe what he has heard is true. He is, after all, distant from the community and unable verify it with his own eyes.

Paul's words in 5:1, "Everyone has heard" or "It is actually reported" (NRSV), might be paraphrased as "I can hardly believe." Paul accentuates his incredulousness by pointing out that the particular type of sexual immorality present is one that "isn't even heard of among the Gentiles" (v. 1). This turn of phrase suggests that it doesn't take a carefully calibrated moral compass to know that this sort of behavior is wrong. Even people who are far removed from the teachings of God understand that it is sinful and corrupt.

The sin in question involves a man who is having a sexual relationship with "his father's wife" (v. 1), that is to say, with his stepmother. By behaving in this way, the man not only commits sin by having sex outside the covenant of marriage, but also breaks the covenant of another's marriage. At the same time, he dishonors his own father and mother by his actions.

Yet the Corinthian community was apparently unfazed by this scandal, much to Paul's chagrin. They seem to have understood the matter as something much less reprehensible than it actually was. Paul makes it clear that the appropriate response to such sin and dysfunction is grief and mourning—not only for the sake of the offender, but also for the sake of the community that has been harmed and warped by the presence of the sin within it.

Up to this point, Paul has been steadily building up his claim to authority in the eyes of the Corinthian believers. He has done so every time he referred to their intimate relationship, called them his "beloved children," named himself as their "father," listed his own sufferings, invited them to be imitators of him, and reminded them that he would be returning. Now, he draws upon all that accumulated authority to establish himself as capable and worthy of pronouncing judgment on the matter "in the name of our Lord Jesus" (v. 4).

Without all the authority upon which he now draws, it would be easy for the Corinthians to discard Paul's judgment as inappropriate. But with the rightfulness of his place among them still fresh in their minds, they can now hear Paul's verdict. They are to exclude the offender from their assembly and "hand this man over to Satan to destroy his human weakness so that his spirit might be saved on the day of the Lord" (v. 5). Only in this way can both the community and the individual be saved.

This was certainly a stunning proclamation to the original audience. Paul has commanded them to

We must not think of "yeast" as the substance that comes in little packets at the grocery store. The more accurate term for what Paul is talking about is "leaven," which is a bit of dough that is pinched off a loaf and kept in a warm, dark place. When yeast, a kind of fungus, develops on it, this bit of dough is kneaded into the next batch to make it rise. For this reason, yeast or leaven is often used in Scripture as a symbol of contamination or uncleanness.

discipline one of their own by removing him from the community itself. As if he can sense their hesitancy, Paul justifies this harsh measure by appealing to a familiar image from domestic life. He asks them, "Don't you know that a tiny grain of yeast makes a whole batch of dough rise?" (v. 6). It seems that Paul wants to impress upon them the impact of sin in the community upon the community itself.

Paul wants to disabuse the Corinthian Christians of any traces of a philosophy that says "live and let live" and thus allows for sin to fester within the church. On the contrary, their community is meant to embody the way of Jesus and the values of the kingdom of God. Paul likens the removal of the man from the community to cleaning out the old yeast so they can be a new batch of dough (v. 7). Sin, Paul says, grows within a community and cannot be ignored or expected just to go away. Instead we must act with honesty and truth (v. 8) and take sin seriously, even—or especially—when it's the sin of one to whom we are committed.

Paul moves from the image of yeast to a clarification of something he had taught the Corinthians before. At some time in the past, Paul had told them "not to associate with sexually immoral people" (5:9), but clarifies that he meant not to associate with "anyone who calls themselves 'brother' or 'sister'" (5:11) who sins openly and unrepentantly.

While conceding that removing oneself from all who sin is impossible, since then they would have to remove themselves completely from the world (v. 10), Paul instructs the church to demand accountability from one of its own. He denies his own right, and consequently the right of the church, to judge those outside the community. "God will judge outsiders," he writes (v. 13). The community, however, must judge itself so that it can remain a

> But if someone has made anyone sad, that person hasn't hurt me but all of you to some degree (not to exaggerate). The punishment handed out by the majority is enough for this person. This is why you should try your best to forgive and to comfort this person now instead, so that this person isn't overwhelmed by too much sorrow. So I encourage you to show your love for this person. (2 Cor 2:5-8)

fellowship of the mutually accountable, forever taking up their crosses to follow "Christ crucified" (1 Cor 1:23).

Understanding

With a topic as challenging as church discipline, we should not leave our passage behind until we are sure that we understand some of the major things that Paul is trying to establish. First, we should carefully study what Paul is telling the Corinthian community to do in terms of what we commonly call church discipline. There is a man in the community who has sinned grievously and unrepentantly and has apparently received some support in his sin from other members of the church. Paul insists that the Corinthian Christians remove this man from their assembly for the protection of the community and for the sake of the man's own salvation. Paul wants this to be not a petty nor vindictive act, but rather a merciful one.

Second, we should not understand this apostolic judgment as an act of punishment. Rather, we must strive to see it instead as a proper recognition of what is already the case. Specifically, the man in question is already separated from the community by virtue of his unrepentant sin. To exclude him now is not to punish him or inflict something upon him, but rather to accurately assess the situation before the eyes of everyone. In essence, the man cannot be reunited with his community until first he recognizes his sin and the separation it has caused.

Third, we must understand the distinction Paul makes between who is and is not accountable to the believing community. The church is charged with judging those who are joined with it and, in doing so, promoting accountability and spiritual formation. It is not, however, the church's role to judge the whole world.

What About Me?

• *We must take sin seriously.* Paul understands sins to be more than those actions arbitrarily forbidden by an inscrutable God. Instead, it seems Paul understands sin to be an infection that warps lives and destroys community. Something this deforming should be taken seriously, both in our own lives and in the lives of those we love and to whom we are committed.

• *Individual sin isn't really individual.* As tempting as it may be to believe that my sin only affects me and is only my business, it clearly has an impact on more than just my own life. After all, my sin separates me from God, and it is God who unites me with my brothers and sisters in Christ. My sin is also the concern of those whom I love and to whom I am committed.

• *If it's not based in love, it's not church discipline.* If we hope to follow Jesus and his ways, then we need to recognize that we can't do it alone, and if we want to do it with others, then we must depend on them to correct us even as we correct them in love. If it's about punishment or some misguided understanding of purity, then it's no longer church discipline—it's something personal.

• *We're not called to judge those who don't ask for it.* Those who join with us in Christian community have submitted themselves to accountability, but those who have yet to join us cannot and should not be held to the same standards.

Resources

Robert Scott Nash, *1 Corinthians*, Smyth & Helwys Bible Commentary (Macon GA: Smyth & Helwys, 2009).

"Stories of the Desert Fathers," *FatherPius.com* <http://www.fatherpius.littleway.ca/desert03.html>.

DEMANDING ACCOUNTABILITY
1 Corinthians 5:1-13

Introduction

There was one situation in the church at Corinth that no one wanted to address. This situation was the classic elephant in the room that everyone in the church tried to pretend wasn't there. But the elephant was there. Paul, never one to mince words, brought the elephant into clear view: "Everyone has heard that there is sexual immorality among you. This is a type of immorality that isn't even heard of among the Gentiles—a man is having sex with his father's wife!" (1 Cor 5:1).

This situation—a man in the church having a sexual relation- ship with his stepmother—was detestable to Paul, so he addressed the issue straight on and told the Corinthians to expel the man from the church. In Paul's mind, that kind of evil was contagious ("a tiny grain of yeast makes a whole batch of dough rise" [v. 6]) and needed to be nipped in the bud before evil took a foothold and the church started spiraling into sin.

These verses point us toward a thorny, tricky topic: church discipline. How can we demand accountability of our fellow church members without becoming critical and mean-spirited? Is it possible to practice church discipline with a spirit of grace? When is it appropriate to speak up about church problems and when should we remain quiet?

All Things New

Paul's demand for accountability among the Corinthian Christians stemmed from his firm conviction that Christian people are different from the world. He later wrote to these Corinthians and said, "So then, if anyone is in Christ, that person is part of the new creation. The old things have gone away, and look, new things have arrived!" (2 Cor 5:17). Paul could make demands of the Corinthians because he believed they had become new and should act like it. To live as if they were not "in Christ" was unacceptable.

When someone makes the decision to follow Jesus Christ, he or she steps into a whole new world. Everything becomes new:

• *A new attitude.* The follower of Christ gets a new attitude—one filled with joy and hope because of the cross and empty tomb. This new attitude is also marked by a desire and willingness to serve others. The change in a person begins on the inside and then manifests itself on the outside.

• *A new purpose.* The follower of Christ also gets a new purpose— partnering with God to build a kingdom of love and grace. The purpose of life becomes more than merely making money or having fun. We invest time and money in building the kingdom of God. This change transforms our day planner and checkbook.

• *A new way of relating to people.* The follower of Christ relates to people with love and grace. If God has related to us with love and grace, shouldn't we do the same for others? If Jesus was willing to wash another's feet, shouldn't we? And if Jesus was willing to die on the cross, shouldn't we be willing to sacrifice at least a little bit ourselves?

The reason Paul was so incensed at the Corinthians for not addressing the sexual immorality in their midst was simple: anyone who was in Christ and had become a new creation would never behave that way. A follower of Christ would have an attitude of love and grace, not lust. A follower of Christ would be focused on building the kingdom of God, not seeking personal pleasure. And a follower of Christ would relate to people—especially a stepmother—with kindness and respect, not sordid exploitation.

It was simply inconceivable to Paul that someone who had stepped into this new world would do something even people in the old world found repulsive.

Guidelines for Church Discipline

That is why Paul confronted the Corinthians. In his typical, blunt way, he told them that the offending man had to be dealt with. "We need to hand this man over to Satan to destroy his human weakness so that his spirit might be saved on the day of the Lord" (1 Cor 5:5). The man needed to be confronted so he might see the light and change his ways. Furthermore, the church needed to confront him to keep his kind of evil from taking root in their midst.

Note how easy it would be to take verses like these and use them to do great harm. These verses could be used to launch us on a modern-day crusade to rid our church of evildoers. Armed with verses like these, we could go on a witch-hunt for sinners in our family of faith. Before we do, however, let's notice a few things about the way Paul confronted the Christians in Corinth, and let's construct some guidelines for church discipline from the way Paul handled this situation.

First, *church discipline must be built on strong evidence*. Paul was dealing with a specific situation in the Corinthian church that was probably common knowledge. When a church member is having a sexual relationship with his stepmother, someone needs to step up and demand repentance.

Too often, however, church discipline takes place without much evidence at all. Someone has suggested that so-and-so might have said such-and-such in a Sunday school class. Or it has been rumored that the pastor is fudging his expense account. Or a deacon has been seen entering a bar late at night. All too often, we go on our church crusades on the basis of rumor and innuendo.

Second, *church discipline must be about substantive issues*. The issue Paul was addressing in Corinth was substantive. Any time a church member is doing something blatantly illegal or immoral, that person needs to be confronted—for his sake and the sake of the church.

But church discipline is not about differences of opinion. Church members can and will disagree on certain points of doctrine, certain items in the church budget, and certain styles of music and worship. But those differences of opinion are just that: differences of opinion. Just because we disagree with a person about such things doesn't give us the right to try to discipline that person. He or she has done nothing illegal or immoral and needs to be left alone. Most witch-hunts in the church are about fairly trivial issues.

Third, *church discipline is to be done with mourning, not anger*. The Greek word Paul uses to describe the kind of attitude he wants the Corinthians to have (which is translated "being so upset" in verse 2), is one that was used to describe mourning for the dead. In other words, when the Corinthians confronted this man, they were not to have a spirit of anger and vindictiveness. They were to come to the confrontation as one approaches a bereaved person. The confrontation was not to be hard and heated but gentle and sympathetic.

Too much church discipline takes place in the midst of anger. People get mad at one another and start lashing out. This kind of confrontation only produces hard feelings and further estrangement. When we approach people with mourning and genuine concern, however, a different dynamic appears and genuine healing can sometimes take place.

Fourth, *the goal of church discipline is restoration*. When we have to confront a fellow believer, we do so with the hope that that person will see the light, repent, and move in a more positive direction. The ultimate goal of the confrontation is restoration, both in the individual's life and with regard to the integrity of the church itself.

What that means, of course, is that church discipline is not about punishment. We're not mad at people and trying to hurt them. We're sad and trying to help. As Paul put it to the Galatian church, "Brothers and sisters, if a person is caught doing something wrong, you who are spiritual should restore someone like this with a spirit of gentleness" (Gal 6:1). Gently restoring people is a far cry from angrily removing them from the church rolls because they don't measure up to our standards.

Paul applied these four principles in his dealings with the Corinthians, and we can do the same today when we have to face difficult situations in our church. If we (1) have strong evidence (2) about substantive issues and (3) can approach people with mourning (4) in an attempt to restore them to wholeness, we might have a chance to redeem a tough situation. If we can't manage these four qualities, though, we should leave church discipline to someone who can.

Sooner Rather than Later

We can save ourselves a lot of pain if we deal with church issues sooner rather than later. The best time to deal with a problem is when it first surfaces. If it has time to fester and eventually become the elephant in the room, it is much more difficult to address.

If only we had talked to the church secretary when we first sensed she was unhappy in her job, we might not be dealing with her termination now. If only the church staff had gone out to eat each week after the staff meeting, we might not be at each other's throats right now. If only we had called our friend when we first thought she was upset with us, we might not be estranged now. If only.... If only....

In his book *The Pursuit of WOW* (New York: Vintage, 1994), Tom Peters writes, "Believe me on this: Most of the mistakes you will make in your career (and probably in your personal life) will come from having avoided that four-minute phone call that could have stopped the farmhand from letting out the cow that kicked over the lantern that started the fire that burned down the barn...." (51).

That is true of most church conflict. If we take care of the little problems early, we can avoid bigger problems later on. Had the Corinthians confronted this man when the problem was first revealed, they might have saved him—and all of them—a lot of pain.

When it comes to conflict and confrontation, an ounce of prevention is worth far more than a pound of cure.

Conclusion

The Bible never tells us the outcome of this dispute. Perhaps the Corinthians ignored Paul's advice and never addressed the issue.

Or perhaps they went to the man in anger and made the situation even worse.

But for a moment, let's think positively and assume the best. Let's assume the Corinthians read Paul's advice about this situation in their church and said, "You know, he's right. We've known this was going on for a long time and have been afraid to speak of it. But for this man's sake, for the sake of his stepmother, and for the sake of the church, let's deal with it and try to get things right."

Let's imagine them approaching the man with a spirit of mourning and speaking to him in love as they tried to help him. Then the man's heart was pierced, and he knew he had been doing wrong. He confessed his sin, sought the forgiveness of all he had offended, and eventually was reinstated in the church. As painful as the ordeal was, the story had a happy ending. The man's life was saved, his family relationships were restored, and the church was able to claim its role as people in Christ who were following his new way.

Wouldn't it be wonderful if the story ended that way? We can only hope. But sadly, most church conflicts don't end that well. Most church conflicts end with hurt feelings, severed relationships, and, occasionally, one group stomping off mad to establish a new church down the road. "We are one in the Spirit, we are one in the Lord" turns out to be only a song.

Sometimes, however, church conflict does have a happy ending. Confrontation leads to reconciliation. Problems have solutions. And people who were at odds with one another join hands and hearts once again to build the kingdom of God.

Notes

Notes

RESOLVING CONFLICTS
MATURELY
1 Corinthians 6:1-8

Central Question

How should I seek justice when I have been wronged?

Scripture

1 Corinthians 6:1-8 When someone in your assembly has a legal case against another member, do they dare to take it to court to be judged by people who aren't just, instead of by God's people? 2 Or don't you know that God's people will judge the world? If the world is to be judged by you, are you incompetent to judge trivial cases? 3 Don't you know that we will judge angels? Why not ordinary things? 4 So then if you have ordinary lawsuits, do you appoint people as judges who aren't respected by the church? 5 I'm saying this because you should be ashamed of yourselves! Isn't there one person among you who is wise enough to pass judgment between believers? 6 But instead, does a brother or sister have a lawsuit against another brother or sister, and do they do this in front of unbelievers? 7 The fact that you have lawsuits against each other means that you've already lost your case. Why not be wronged instead? Why not be cheated? 8 But instead you are doing wrong and cheating—and you're doing it to your own brothers and sisters.

Reflecting

"A conflicted church," a dear friend once told me, "is a powerful thing." I assumed he must have misspoken. Perhaps he meant to say a "united church" or a "missional church," so I interrupted him to ask him to say that again. After all, this was a man whose opinion I respected deeply, and who had a certain amount of wisdom when it came to church matters. He repeated himself with a smile, "A conflicted church is a powerful thing."

Having my full and undivided attention (and my confused and incredulous look), he laid it out for me like this: "Of course a conflicted church is powerful," he started, "because God does strong things with weak tools."

I began to nod my head with him as I started to see where he was going with this. He continued, "A conflicted church that repents of its divisions and is united around Jesus stands out in a world where conflict sends folks scattering. After all," he added, clapping me on the shoulder, "Jesus came for the sick, brother—and some of our congregations are pretty sick. What better proof of God's power is there than a healed bunch of sinners getting along like they love each other?"

> When have you observed the transforming power that can come from being reconciled with another?

I had to admit he had a point. By no means is conflict or disunity within a congregation a good thing, but we do serve a God who does great things with broken instruments.

Each time one of our communities divides itself is an opportunity once again to prove that our God is bigger than even our most ardent disagreements. Jesus assured us, "This is how everyone will know that you are my disciples, when you love each other" (Jn 13:35), but perhaps he could have also said, "When your love for one another conquers whatever separates you, the world will come running."

Studying

In our previous lessons, Paul discussed the disunity within the Corinthian church and pointed out some of the problems these conflicts created. He repeatedly reprimanded the believers in Corinth for their self-obsession and selfishness, and he told them that their divisions and partisanship were signs of spiritual immaturity. The Apostle saw their jealousy, quarreling, and bickering as signs of arrested spiritual development both individually and as a congregation. In short, Paul spent a significant number of words detailing the divisions and brokenness among the Corinthian Christians.

In chapter 5, Paul goes even further in his rebuke by reminding the Corinthian believers of a particular issue within their congregation. A man had been having a sexual relationship with his own stepmother. Although the church was aware of the situation, they failed to correct him, and he remained unrepentant.

Paul commanded the church to exclude this member from its assemblies and not even to eat with such a person. This was meant for the good of both the community and the individual, as it would (Paul hoped) lead him finally to repent and be restored. The Apostle went on to assure the Christians that it was their calling to hold each other accountable within the community, even though they had no right to hold outsiders to the same high standards they embraced for themselves.

All of this was for the sake of the community, both collectively and with respect to its individual members. Having affirmed the need for the church to exercise such judgment and hold its members to a high standard, Paul introduces a related topic in chapter 6. Here, he discusses the appropriate way for a Christian community to resolve its own internal disputes.

This follows quite logically from what comes before in chapter 5. If a community was going to start judging itself and holding its own to accountability, then there most certainly would be conflicts! Then, now, we are a broken people. Even though we are called to model a different way of living, that doesn't mean we won't still make selfish decisions or react defensively to correction. Part of modeling a different way of living to the world is modeling a different way of resolving disputes.

Paul seems shocked to have heard that the Corinthian Christians are taking their disputes to civil judges outside of the community (1 Cor 6:1). It is apparent that he is astonished that they have so obviously misunderstood what he had taught them previously about the need for discipline and accountability. He never meant they should start suing each other in court!

The Corinthian community has chosen to act like the world, however, in spite of their calling to do otherwise. Paul is flummoxed about how they could so fundamentally misunderstand the pattern by which their community was intended to live.

In response, Paul asks them a series of leading questions. These are questions they know how to answer—and they know that Paul knows they know how to answer! This rhetorical tactic is a blunt way of reminding them that they know better. Paul even goes so far as to finish this line of questions with the words, "I'm saying this because you should be ashamed of yourselves!" (1 Cor 6:5).

The content of these questions is that the Corinthian Christians should remember that God's people will judge "the world" (v. 2), that is, the greater world outside the community of believers. Given that Paul had recently said that God would judge the world and that the community should stay out of it (5:13), Paul must mean God's people would judge within the context of God's ultimate judgment. Perhaps he means that God's people would hold positions of honor and authority in the world to come. Paul claims that God's people would even judge angels, so why shouldn't they be granted a measure of authority in judging "ordinary things" (6:3).

Paul then explicitly names the failure that the Corinthian community is committing. They are appealing to worldly authorities to decide community matters. They are competent to resolve their own disputes and, by doing so, demonstrate the power of God and God's love, but they refuse to do what they are able to do. Instead, they have chosen to ask the world and its broken judges for help.

Note that Paul's concern is going before the courts to resolve internal disputes in the congregation. There is no mention of actual civil crimes such as embezzlement, fraud, or sexual assault. Sadly, such things do sometimes happen in churches, and this passage should never be used to prevent the civil authorities from becoming involved when they do.

Therein lies the problem. It seems that members of the Corinthian congregation are taking each other to court to resolve internal disputes and, by so doing, they belie the authority and competency of the church before a broken world.

Paul points out that the conflicts and brokenness that the Corinthian Christians are suffering are painful enough without going before worldly authorities to resolve them. Going a step further, Paul points out that no matter what the verdict in a case of disputes brought before outsiders, it is already a defeat for everyone involved: "The fact that you have lawsuits against each other means that you've already lost your case" (v. 7). Whether justice is served or not, Paul seems to say, the community is further fractured in the eyes of the world.

Paul's solution can be controversial. He asks, "Why not be wronged instead? Why not be cheated?" (v. 7) This is a shocking suggestion to the world, but it makes a peculiar kind of sense given the values of the kingdom of God and the other things Paul has suggested in previous chapters. Paul insists that it would be better for the Christians in Corinth to suffer injustices, wounds, and wrongs from fellow believers than it would be for them to gratify themselves and their desires for vengeance with an illusion of justice. It would be best, the Apostle says, if everyone in the community were ruled by love. But if it isn't possible for love to rule them all, it can at least rule the one who has been wronged. And that is better than love ruling none of them.

As if discouraged by the conduct of the self-seeking and self-concerned Corinthian Christians, Paul concludes, "But instead you are doing wrong and cheating—and you're doing it to your own brothers and sisters" (v. 8). It would seem that the divisions run so deeply within this community that the love that should unite it has given way to a vain pursuit of an eye for an eye and retributive justice. In future passages, Paul will try to break his beloved Corinthian brothers and sisters of this mindset.

Understanding

With a challenging passage like this one, we should be careful what conclusions we draw from it and what conclusions we ignore as "too idealistic." First, we should understand at the outset that Paul is speaking about internal disputes and interpersonal conflicts within the congregation or community. This passage is not about criminal offenses. When speaking of such (abuse, embezzling, adultery, etc.), some have misused this passage to manipulate a congregation into not doing what it should. We should never forget that this passage comes on the heels of another passage that tells us how to deal with weightier offenses and matters.

Second, we should understand the implications of Paul's astonishing declaration about the church's place in judging the world and even the angels. This is no small thing! God will invite us to participate in the correcting and reforming of the world in which we have lived when it comes time to heal all of the broken things that plague us. Who knows better the pain of what is broken in our world than those who have participated in it? This world is not the world that will be, and we who have learned what is good by following Jesus in the community he established will have a hand in refashioning it.

Third, we should not understand Paul's admonition to suffer wrongs and be defrauded as a command not to seek justice or to welcome abuse. Rather, we should see this passage for what it is: a proclamation of the power of love to conquer even those who hurt us and hate us. Turning the other cheek, praying for our persecutors, and loving our enemies is not about getting walked on. It's about swallowing up evil in love and refusing to respond in kind so our enemies will see their actions for the evil they are.

> Darkness cannot drive out darkness; only light can do that. Hate cannot drive out hate; only love can do that.
> —Martin Luther King Jr.

What About Me?

• *We are competent to resolve our own internal disputes.* After all, if we're called by God to be the salt and light of the world in which we live, then what challenge are disagreements and arguments to us? The source of our power to be united is devotion to the same Lord and the practice of unconditional and non-coercive love within our communities.

• *How we choose to resolve internal disputes says something about whom we trust.* When we depend on worldly authorities and powers to resolve the tensions and anxieties that occur between us and our brothers and sisters in Christ, we proclaim to the world that love does not rule in our midst. When we cover over sins with our love, we testify about a God whose love is big enough to save the world.

• *Our love is a sign to the world of God's love.* Every time we offer grace, mercy, love, or forgiveness to another, we are advancing the kingdom of God in our midst and demonstrating a different way of living and approaching life. When love flourishes, our God— who *is* love—moves in that place and in that moment in a powerful way.

• *It's better to suffer than to cause others to suffer.* The cycles of violence and suffering are prolonged when we live by an ethic of an eye for an eye. Rather, we need to believe, and proclaim by our actions, that the cycles of sin and injury can and should end with us, swallowed up by our love and God's love.

Resource

Robert Scott Nash, *1 Corinthians*, Smyth & Helwys Bible Commentary (Macon GA: Smyth & Helwys, 2009).

...dom of the World

...uick reading of 1 Corinthians makes it obvious that Paul
...impressed with the wisdom of the world. In chapter 1, he
... clear that the wisdom of God and the wisdom of the
...e at cross-purposes.

...n Paul heard that the Corinthians were having their
... adjudicated by the wisdom of the world, he was incredu-
...Cor 6:1). Why would people called together by God and
...od's Spirit stoop to seek the wisdom of the secular

...e was a common thought among Jews during this time
...he golden age to come, God would judge the nations, and
...ts would assist God in that judgment. A line from the
...hal Wisdom of Solomon refers to this judging responsi-
...' the saints and says, "The godly will judge nations and
...wer over peoples" (Wis 3:8). In this lesson's Scripture,
...s why God's people would choose to be judged by the
...eous if they themselves were going to one day judge the
...orld, and even the angels.
... counseled them to work out their disputes internally. He
...l there was enough wisdom within the church to handle
...flict: "Isn't there one person among you who is wise
... to pass judgment between believers?" (1 Cor 6:5). If the
...did not have that kind of wisdom, or if it would not use
...d of wisdom, Paul had one word to describe the situation:
...ul. It was a crying shame if the church was so unwise it
...urn to the spurious wisdom of the world to resolve its
...s.
...'s contention that the church should solve its own
...s was built on some definite convictions. Namely, Paul
...l that when people come to Christ...

...nter a new world that is foreign to secular people.
...eceive the Holy Spirit, the giver of wisdom and guidance.
...ecome part of the church, a community united by a
...n purpose that the world at large does not share or under-

RESOLVI

Even a c
was not
makes i
world a

Whe
dispute
lous (1
led by C
world?

The
that in
the sair
apocry
bility o
hold po
Paul as
unrigh
whole

Pau
believe
the con
enough
church
that ki
shame.
had to
disput

Pau
disput
believe

• They
• They
• They
comm
stand.

Introduction

The first church I pastored was a small, cou
Texas. On a "big Sunday," we would have fc
school and sixty for morning worship. The
make ends meet and paid us a modest fifty-
But we loved the members, and they treatec
were a lot of tears shed when we left.

A short time after we left, the church en
The new pastor did some things that riled u
and soon the church had clearly defined pro
pastor groups. After months of wrangling, t
decided it had had enough and bolted. They
just a few miles from the old one.

Here was a fine church of wonderful peo
along. They could barely survive financially
could they hope to survive as two? It was a l
situation.

We would like to think this was a sad abe
been in churches long enough, we know tha
is that churches fight. Sometimes they split.
churches can so spiral out of control that me
and bring charges against one another. That'
in the church at Corinth. Things like this sti
far as I know, no one in that little church in
went to court, but I know it does happen. W
a statement to the world we Christians woul

• They start to live by grace, not law. The old ethic of an eye for an eye and a tooth for a tooth is gone, and a new way of grace begins.

I think it is fair to say that anyone who has those convictions will conclude as Paul did. It makes no sense to take your fellow Christians to court if you believe those four things. Why seek the wisdom of the world when the world doesn't understand your priorities and standards at all? Why seek the wisdom of the world if you already have the Holy Spirit, the Spirit of Truth, within you? Why seek the wisdom of the world if you have the church, a community where people do understand you and share your passion and purpose? And why seek the wisdom of the world if you know about grace, while the world knows only about law?

Paul's understanding of church life was anchored to those four convictions. They guided him resolutely into clear counsel to the Corinthians: solve your disputes internally, since there is more wisdom in the church than in the world.

Witness to the World

Paul was not only concerned about the inner workings of the Corinthian church. He was also concerned about the influence the inner workings of the church would exert on the secular world. "Outsiders" were closely watching the fledgling Christian movement, and Paul knew they would form an impression of the church by the way Christians treated one another.

Why would anyone be attracted to the Christian Way if it was a way of arguing, fighting, and marching in anger to the courtroom? The world at large was already a place of arguing, fighting, and legal wrangling. Who in Corinth needed more of that?

Before we launch into our modern-day arguments, fights, and legal disputes, those of us in the church need to consider what we're saying to the outside world, too. In a world where people face anger and contention in nearly every arena of their lives, shouldn't there be one place where people get along? Shouldn't the church be an oasis in a sea of wrangling? When church members do disagree, shouldn't they handle their disputes both honestly and graciously? Shouldn't the church be a model to the world on how to handle conflict?

Whenever the church chooses to handle its disputes internally with both honesty and grace, it makes a statement to the world, the very statement Paul wanted the Corinthians to make about who Christians are:

• We live in a new world, a world quite unlike the "outside" world.
• We are guided by the Holy Spirit, a gift from God to give discernment and wisdom.
• We have banded together to form the church and even when we disagree, we can handle our disagreements with respect and kindness.
• We have learned the way of grace, so we don't deal with our disputes only by law.

Though those convictions are rarely articulated, they are clearly seen any time a church chooses to handle its conflicts internally and does so with integrity and respect for one another. Each of us must ask what our church is saying to the world in the way it handles conflict.

No Power Struggles

Beyond the lawsuits in the church at Corinth, Paul saw a deeper problem. The conflict and ensuing lawsuits were prompted by a spirit of revenge and a desire to win a power struggle: "The fact that you have lawsuits against each other means that you've already lost your case. Why not be wronged instead? Why not be cheated? But instead you are doing wrong and cheating—and you're doing it to your own brothers and sisters" (vv. 7-8).

Paul's thinking went something like this: Do you really have to win at all costs? When you have disagreements in the church, do you have to get your way, regardless of the damage you do to the church's unity and witness? Instead of damaging your church, why don't you just swallow your pride and be wronged? Instead of hurting your church's witness to the world, why don't you just agree to be defrauded? Being wronged is much better than damaging your church, and being defrauded is much better than hurting your church's witness to the world.

What Paul was saying to the Corinthians is a word we need to hear too, especially if we're having conflict in our own church. The message is, as the saying goes, "It's not about you." It's not about your power, your rights, and your opinion. Give up a preoccupation with those things and let yourself be wronged and defrauded. Admit that this conflict is really a power struggle, and decide to drop out of it.

If we could do that, most church squabbles would disappear. Without power struggles, issues can be handled honestly and graciously. When people no longer demand their rights and their power, walls disappear and bridges are built. The welfare of the church starts to take precedence over personal issues and feelings.

Even as I write this, though, I know how hard it is to do. It's one thing to say we shouldn't have power struggles in the church, but it's another thing altogether to give up my personal power and let someone else win. After all, shouldn't the "right" side win in this battle? And are we just going to stand by while someone defrauds us?

Paul says that's exactly what we should do. Give up our power. Be wronged. Get defrauded. This issue in the church will never be resolved until someone breaks the cycle of conflict and retaliation. Demanding my rights and asserting my power will always get in the way of harmony and reconciliation.

Conclusion

Perhaps that is the best place to end this unit on church conflict. For five lessons now, we've agonized our way through this painful section in 1 Corinthians, in which Paul tries to help the Corinthians deal with the conflict in their midst.

• Paul reminded them about the character of God, made most visible in Jesus' death on the cross. He gave them a theological basis for dealing with church conflict in a spirit of humility and grace.
• Paul wrote to them about factions in the church and how those factions kept them from working together to build the kingdom of God.

• Paul told them to lead by example, even as he had, and he sent Timothy to them to be a flesh-and-blood model of peace and reconciliation.
• Paul reminded them that the church was a community where sexual immorality was not permitted and gave them counsel on how to handle a hard situation.
• Paul encouraged them to resolve their disputes internally without going to the outside world for justice.

Paul's counsel to the Corinthians addressed specific situations in that church. If Paul were writing to our church today, he would no doubt address different situations. But the basic principles he laid down for the Corinthians over 2,000 years ago still make good sense.

We still need to remember the gracious, sacrificing character of God and try to emulate it. We still need to get rid of factions in our church and work together to build the kingdom. We still need to be examples of peace and grace and remember that what we *do* in the midst of church conflict speaks louder than what we *say*. We still need to confront situations in the church that compromise the way of Christ, but in a way that heals and restores. And we still need to resolve our disputes internally without having to go to the courtroom.

Undergirding all of those principles is the attitude Paul commended to the Corinthians in this final study—a spirit that takes the focus off of *me* and puts it on *us*. If our churches can ever have a serving spirit that is willing to lose and be defrauded, power struggles will vanish and so will the conflict those power struggles produce.

Let it be, Lord. Let it be.

Notes

Notes

www.ingramcontent.com/pod-product-compliance
Lightning Source LLC
Chambersburg PA
CBHW070551030426
42337CB00016B/2452